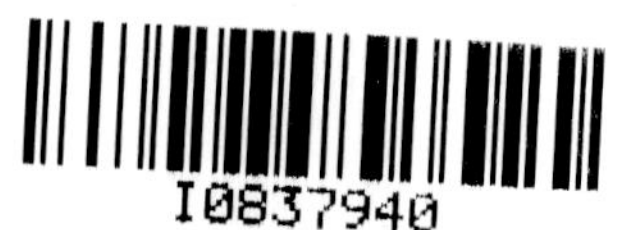

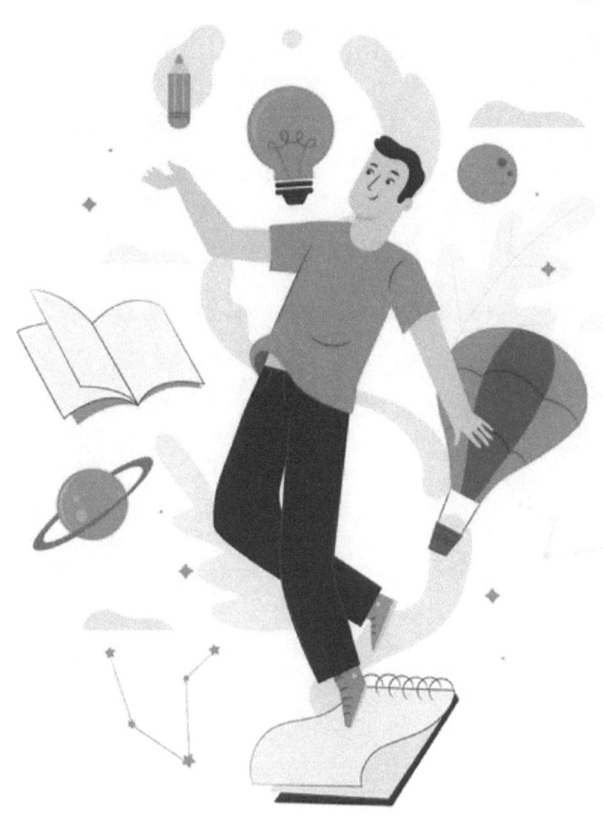

This coloring book belongs to:

____

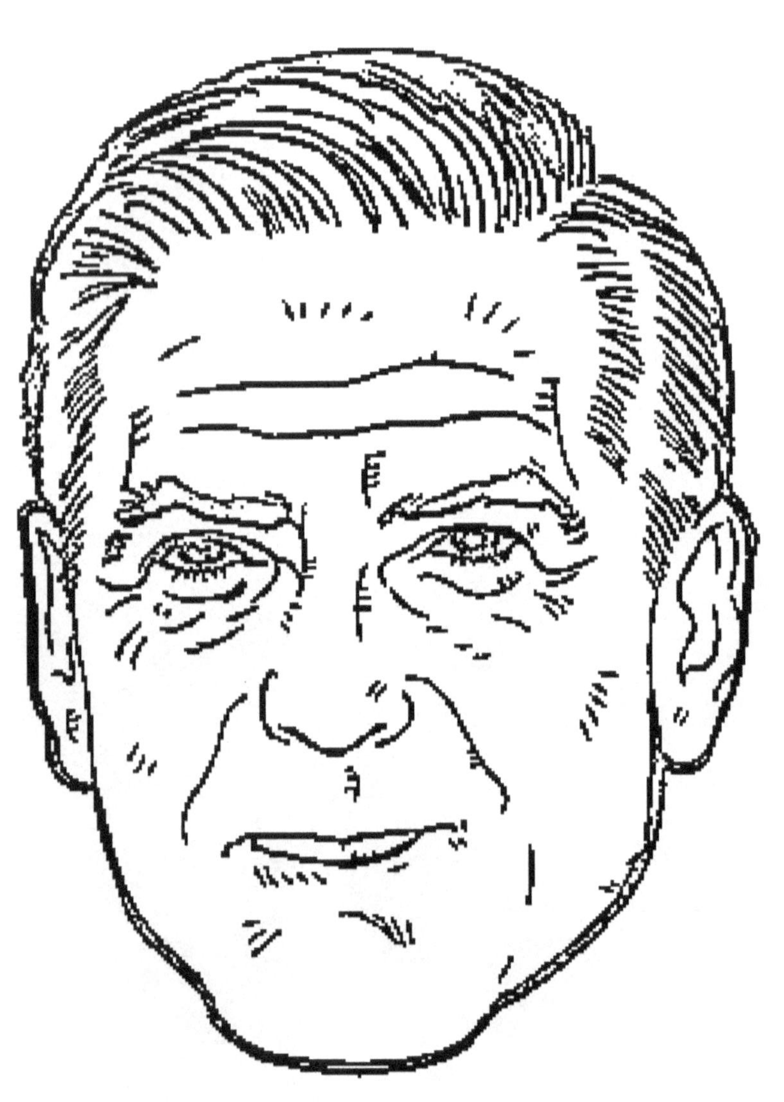

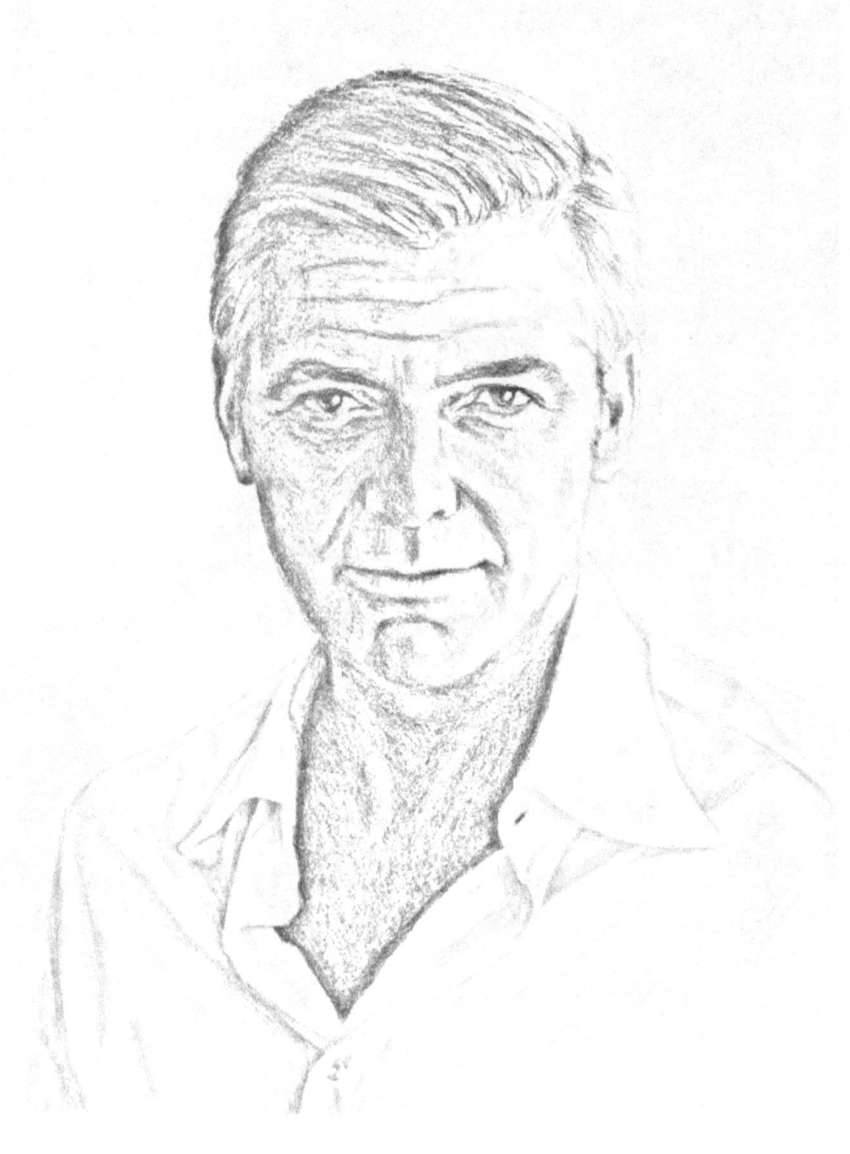

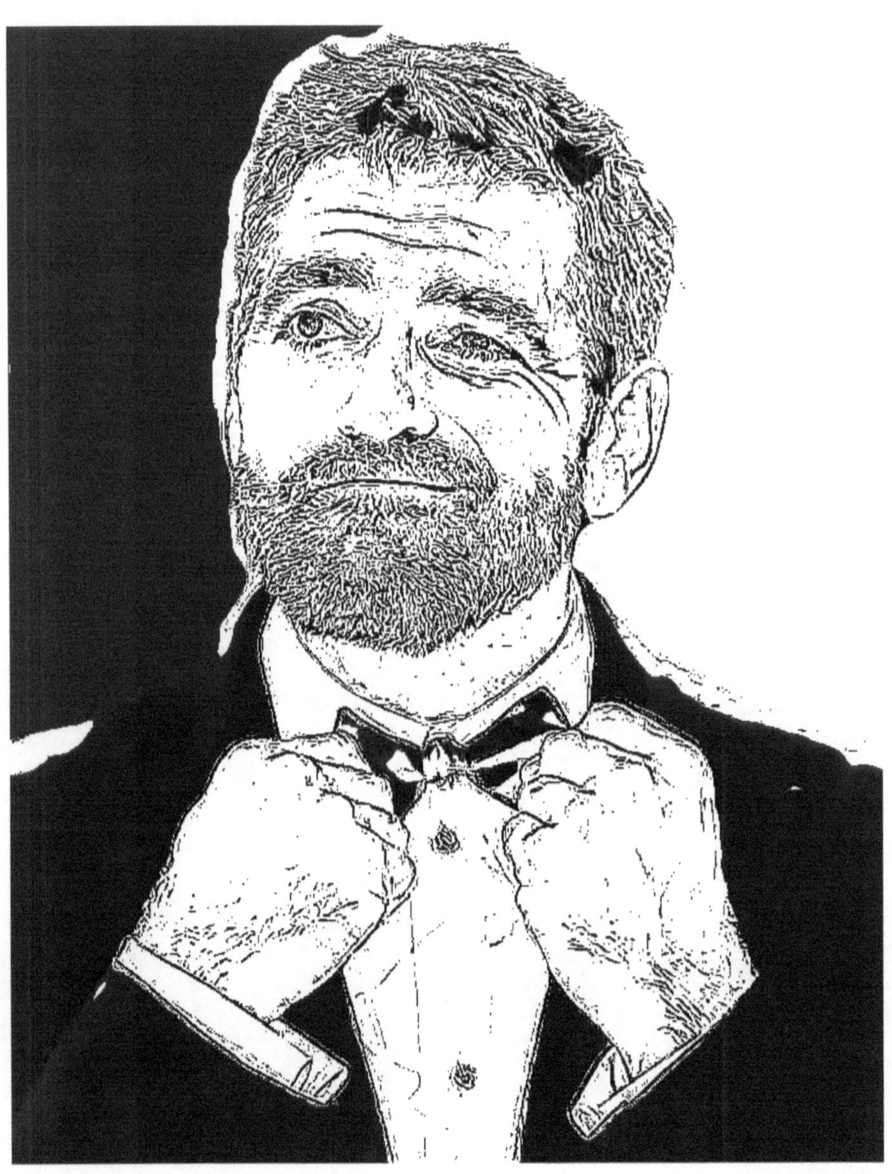

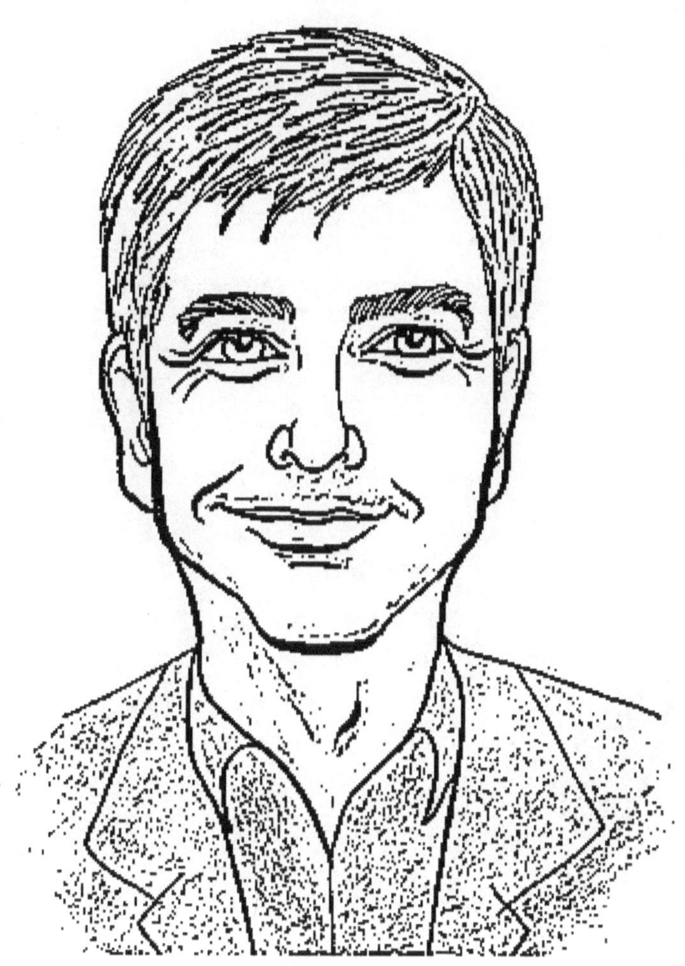

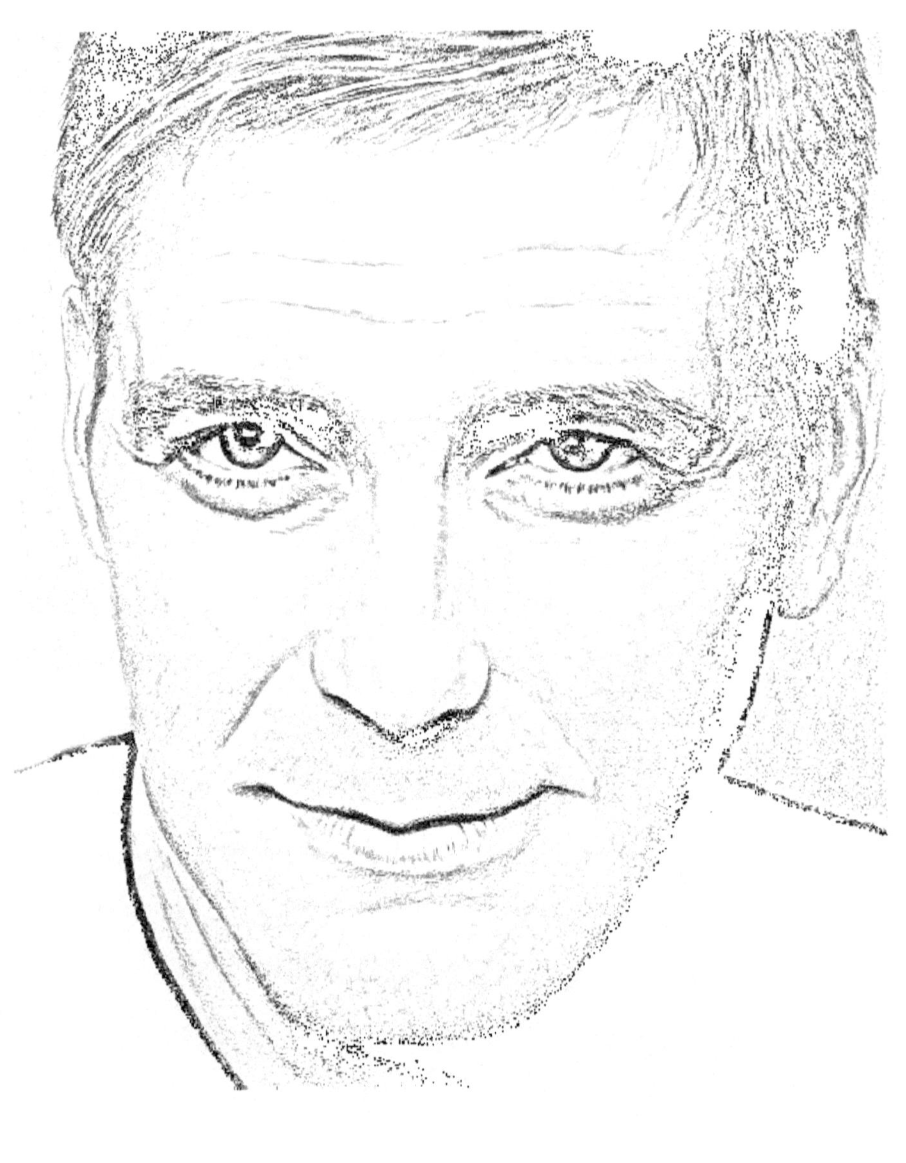

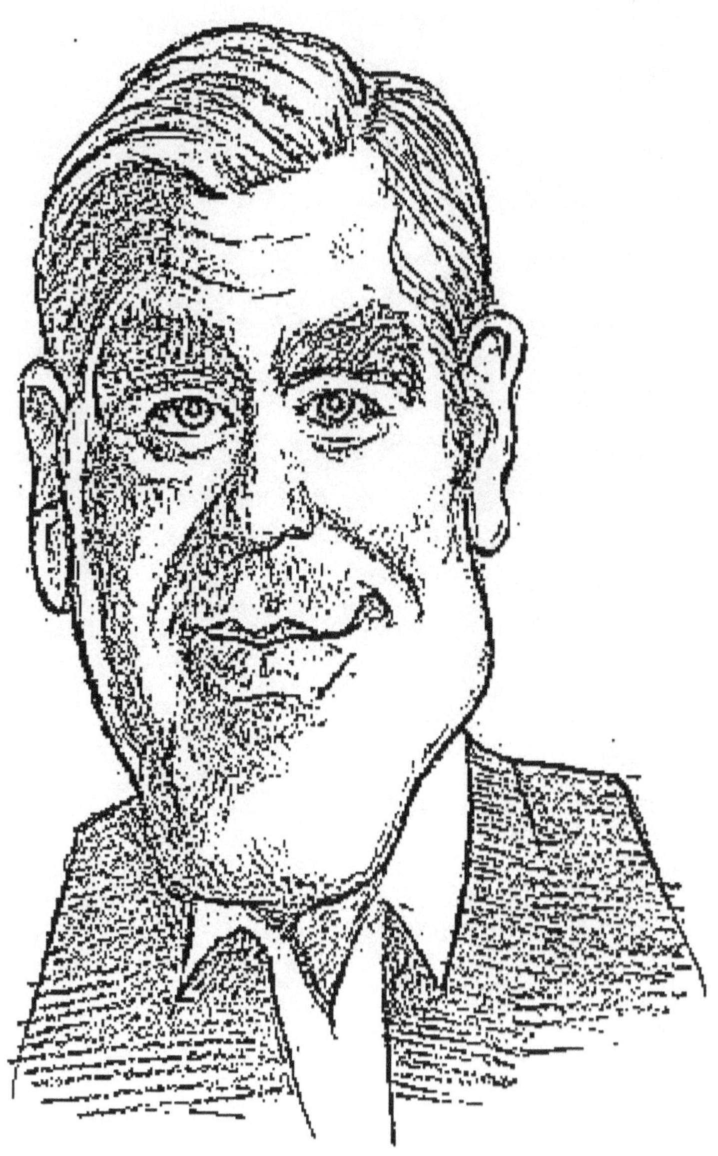

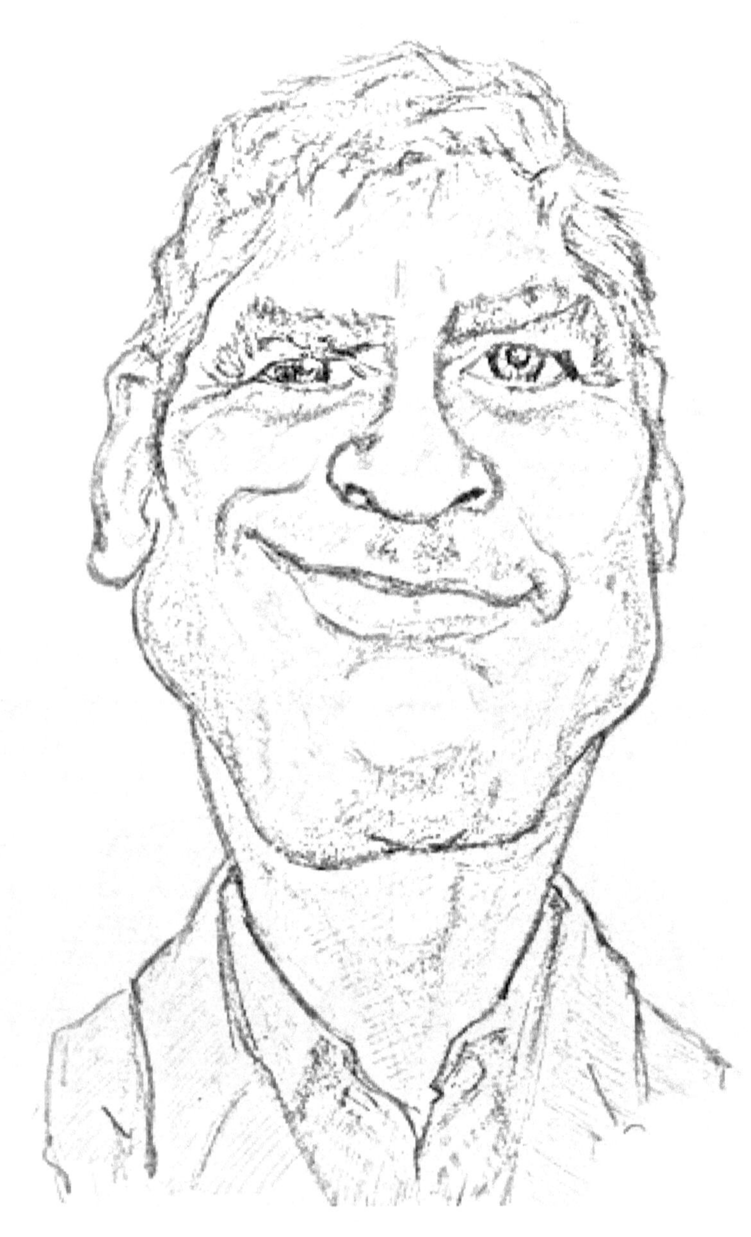

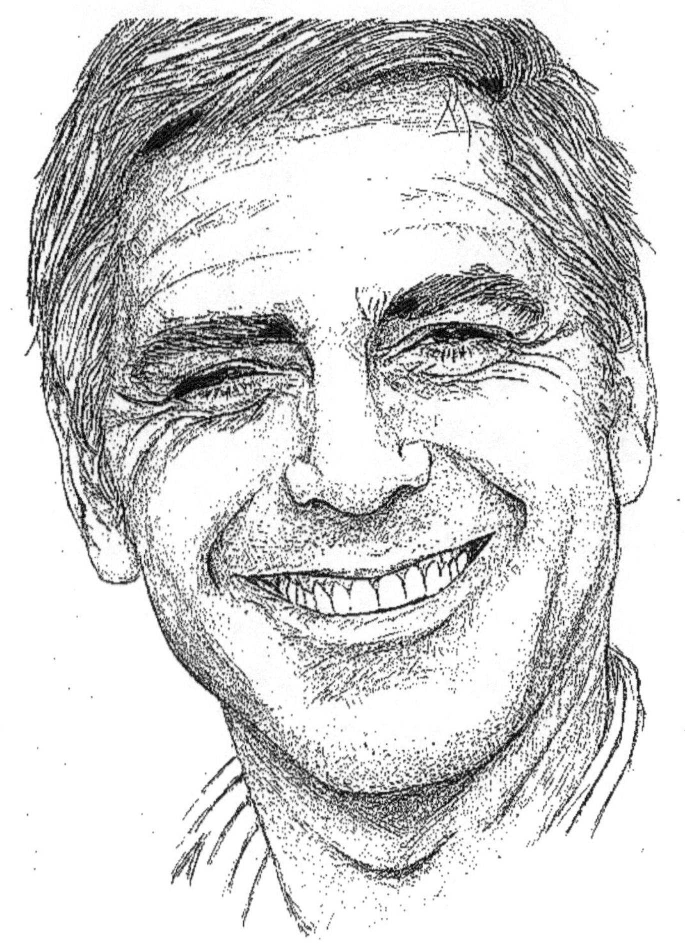

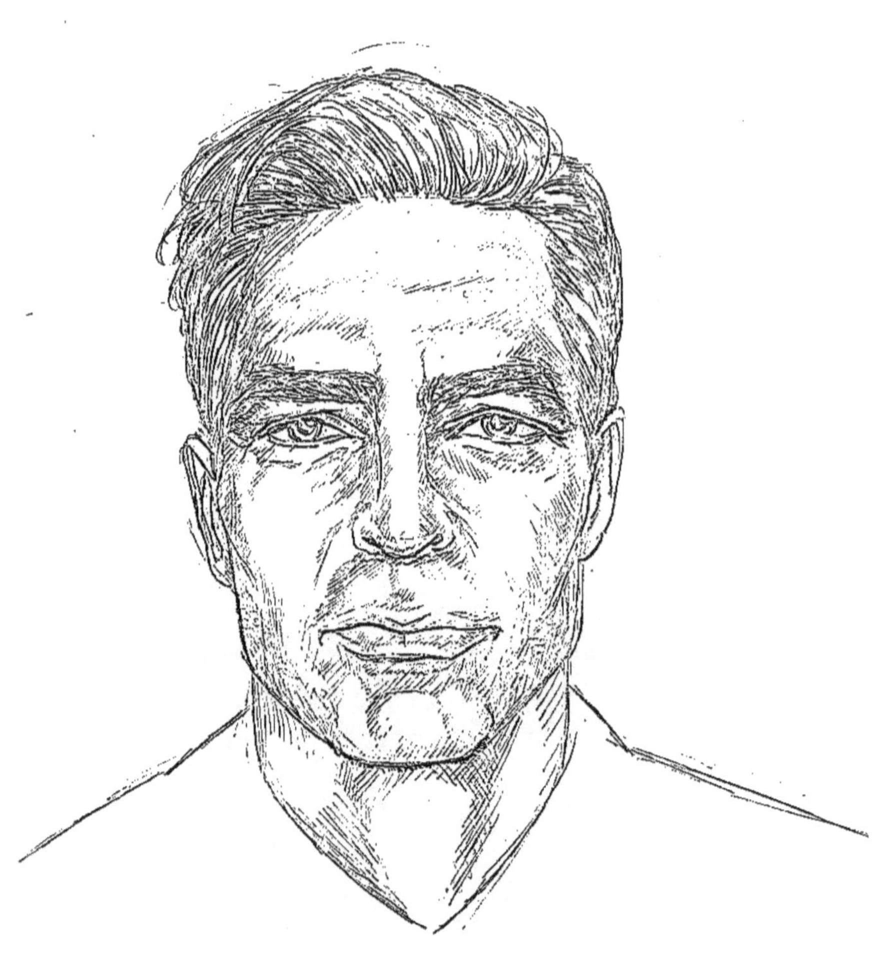

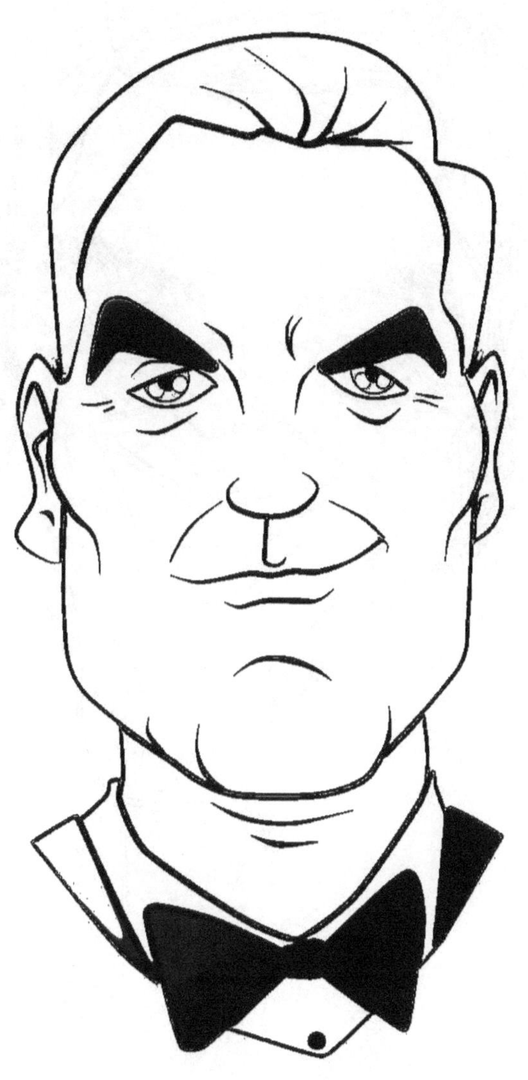

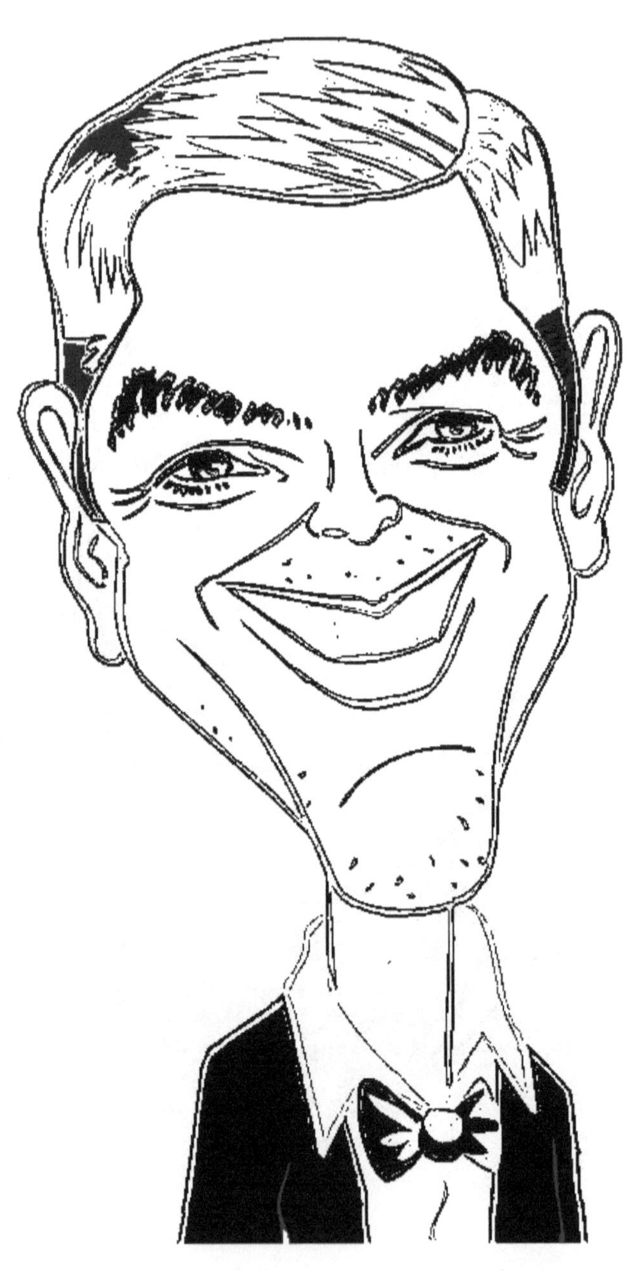

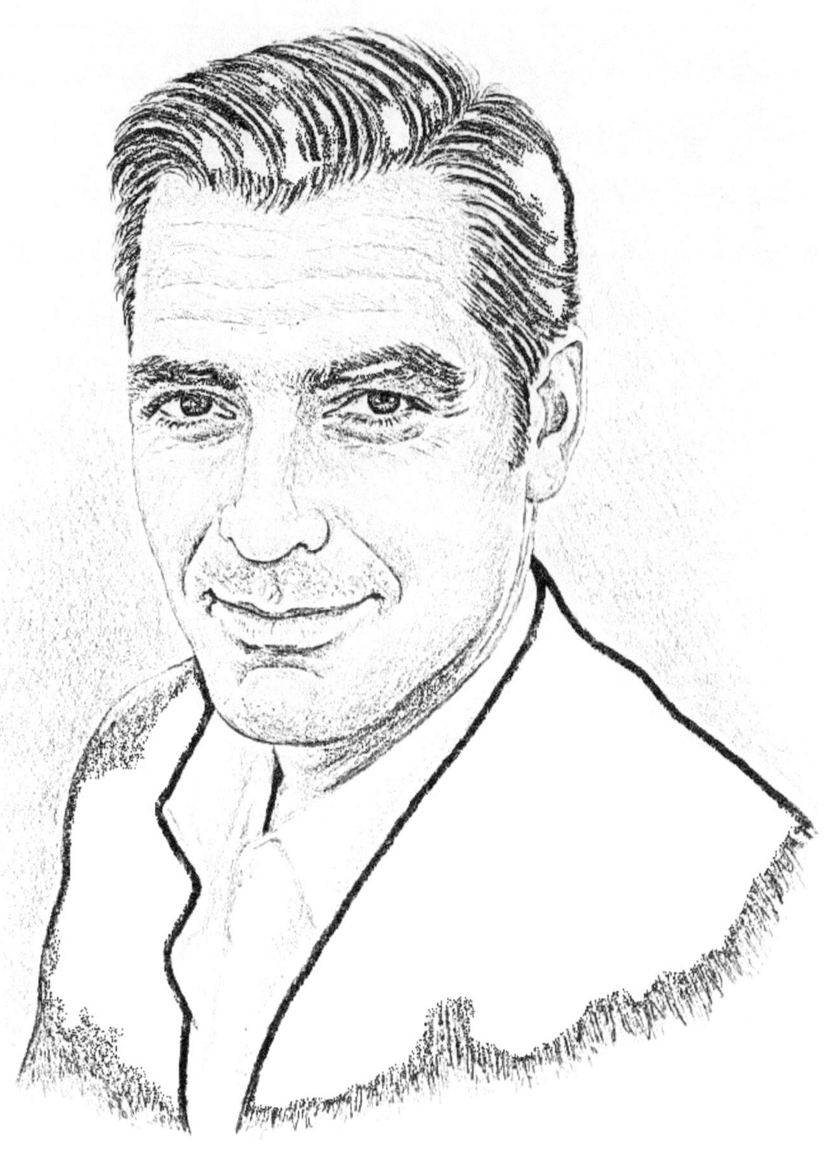

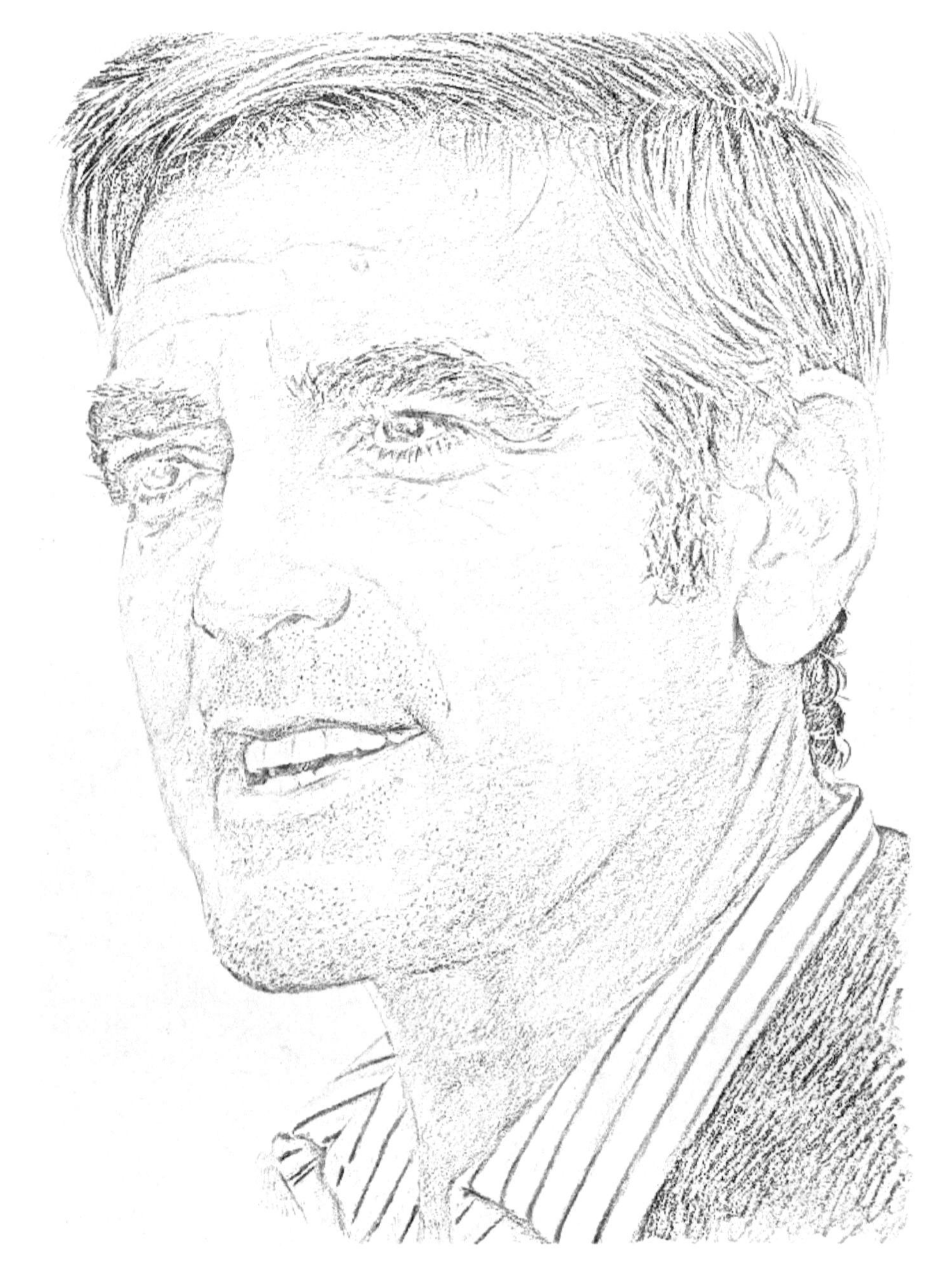

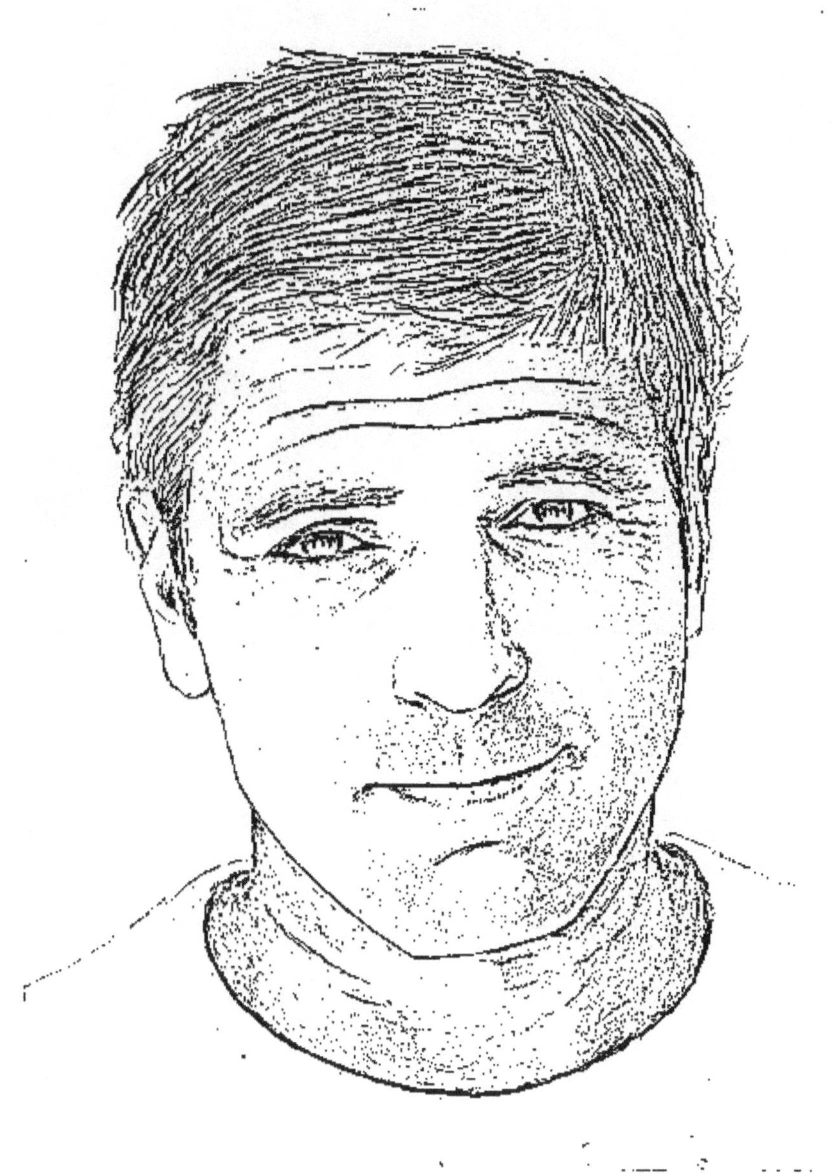

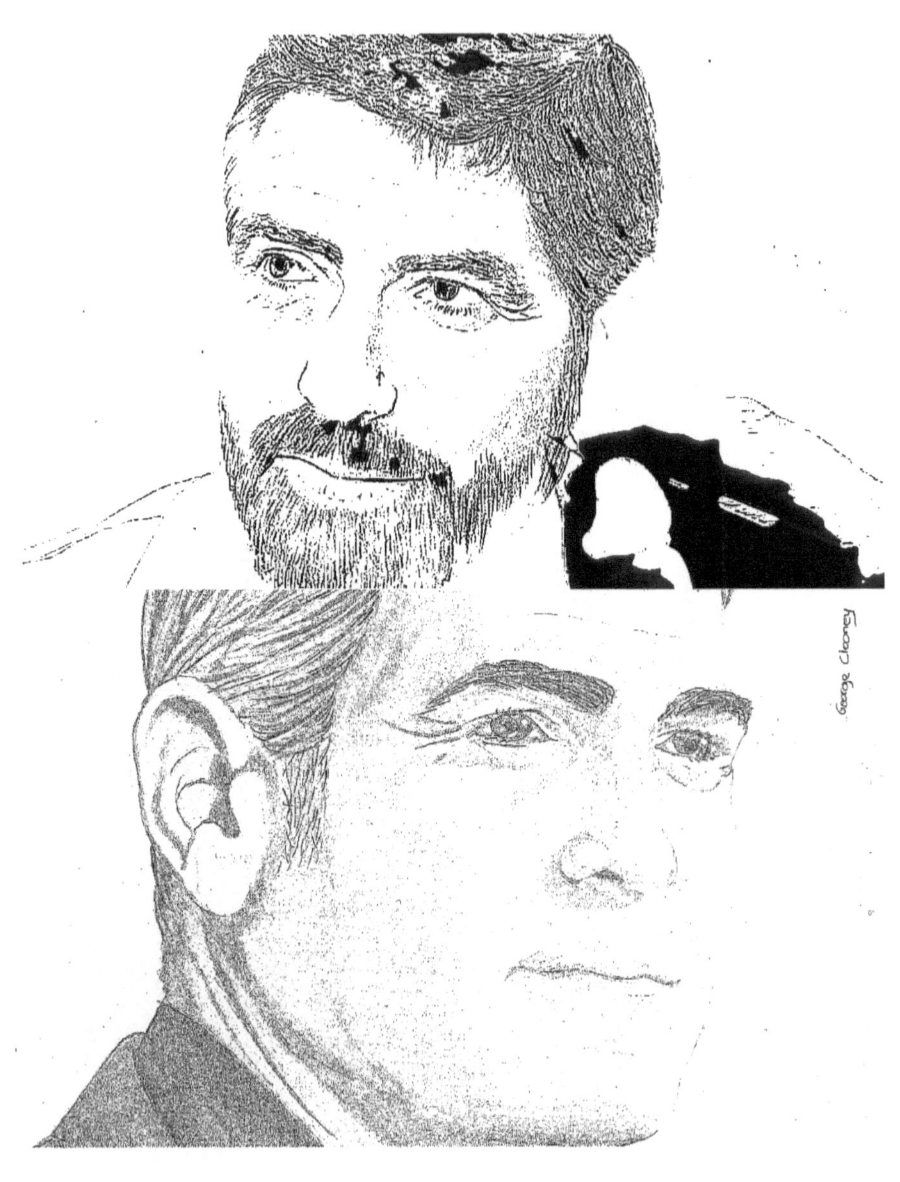

George Clooney

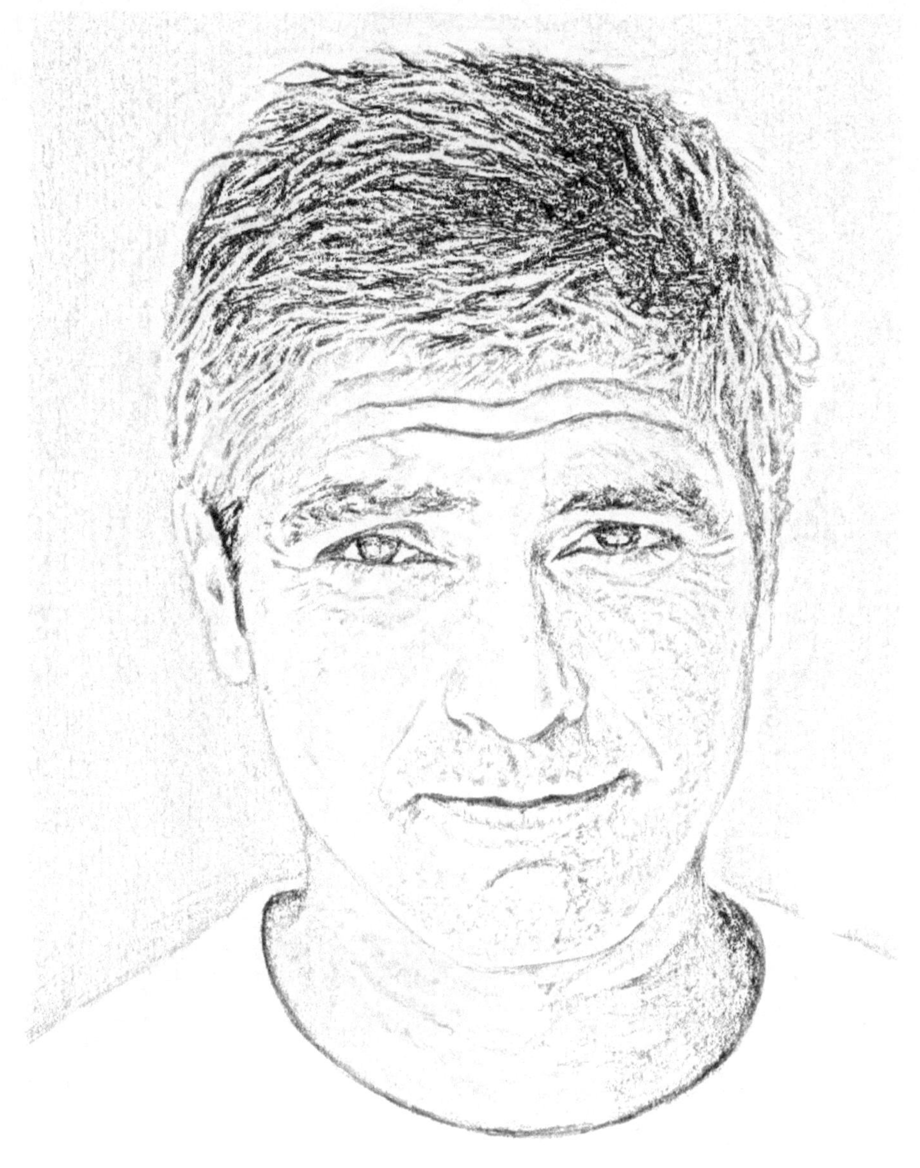

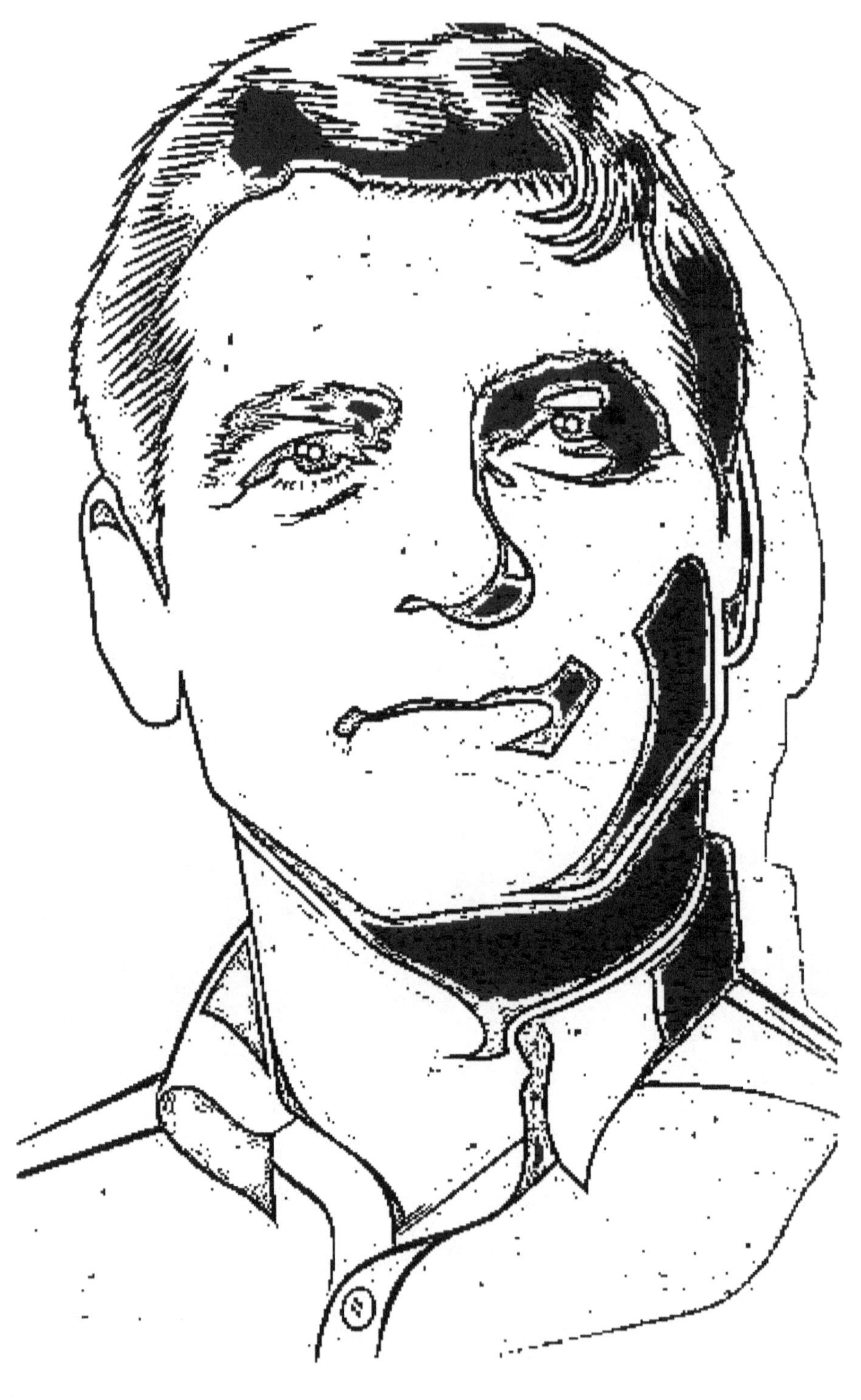

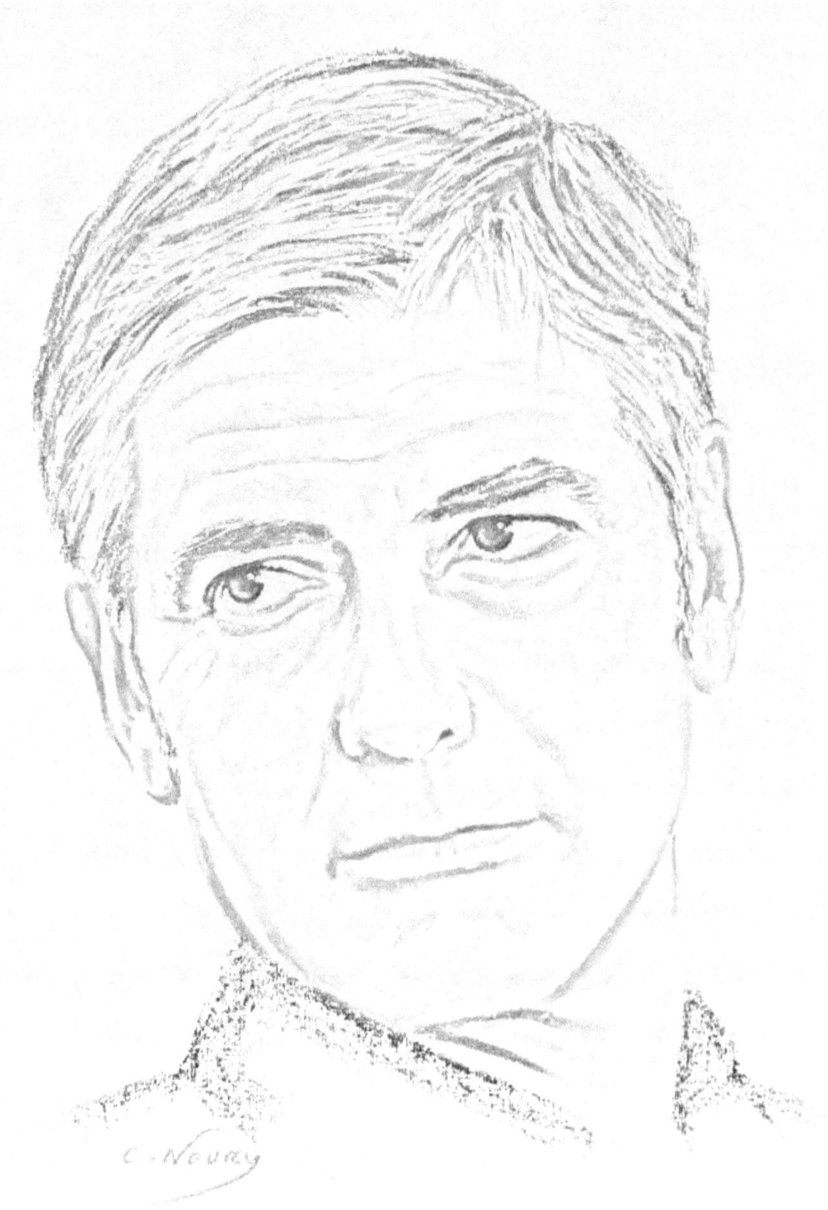

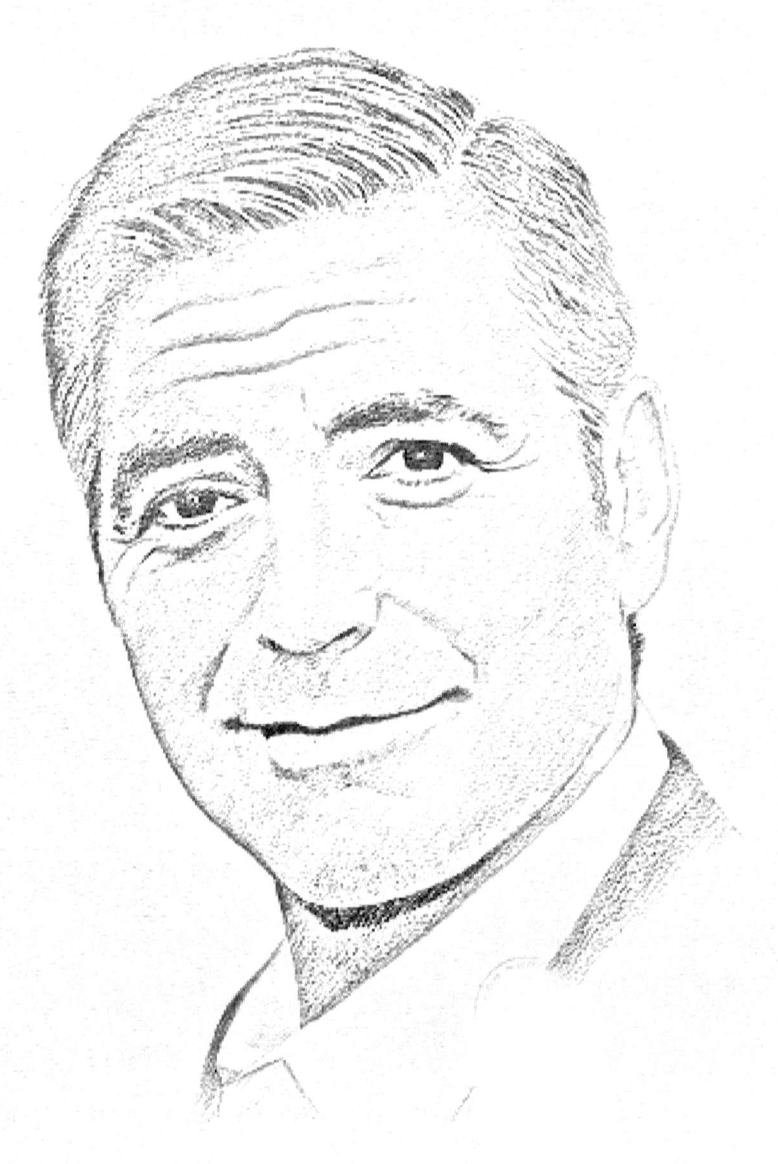

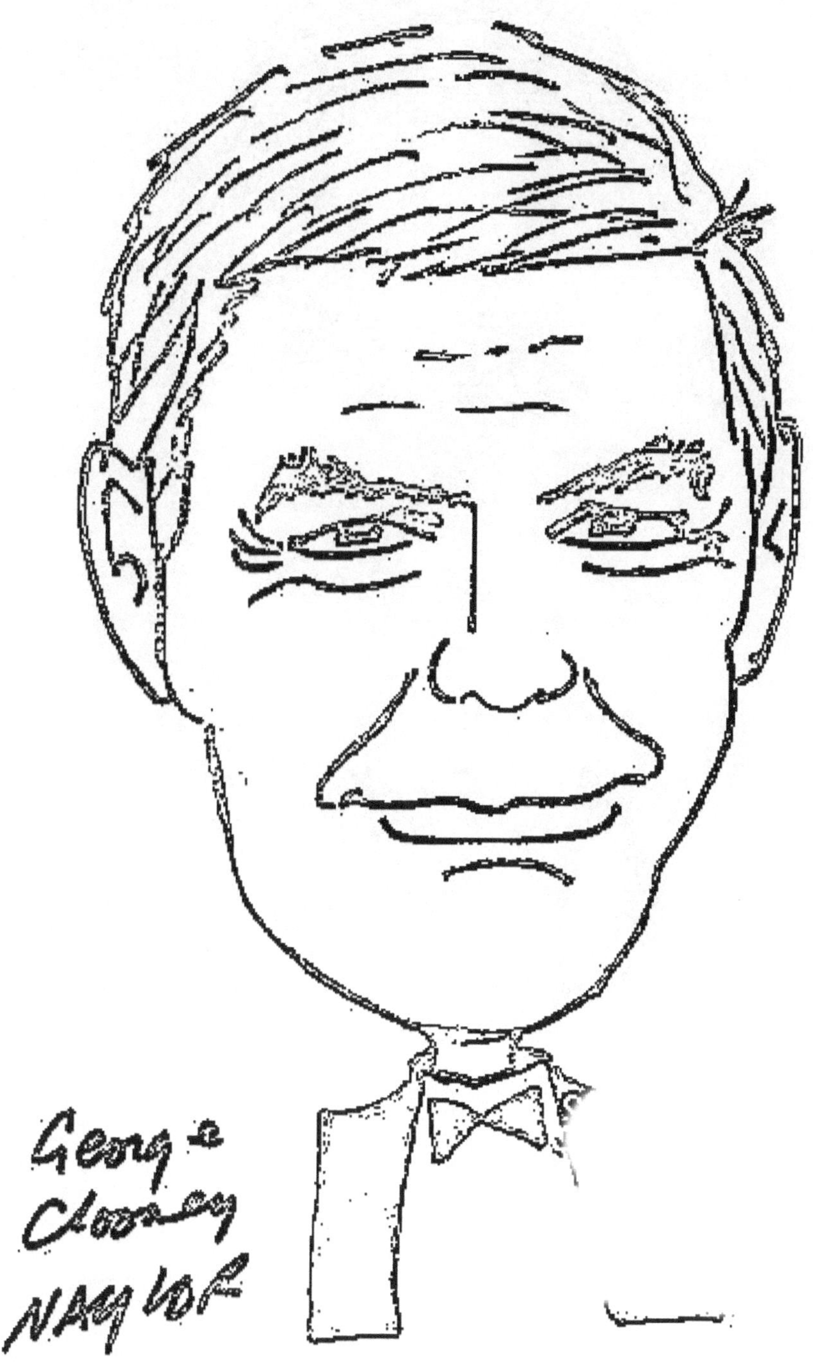

George
Clooney
NAYLOR

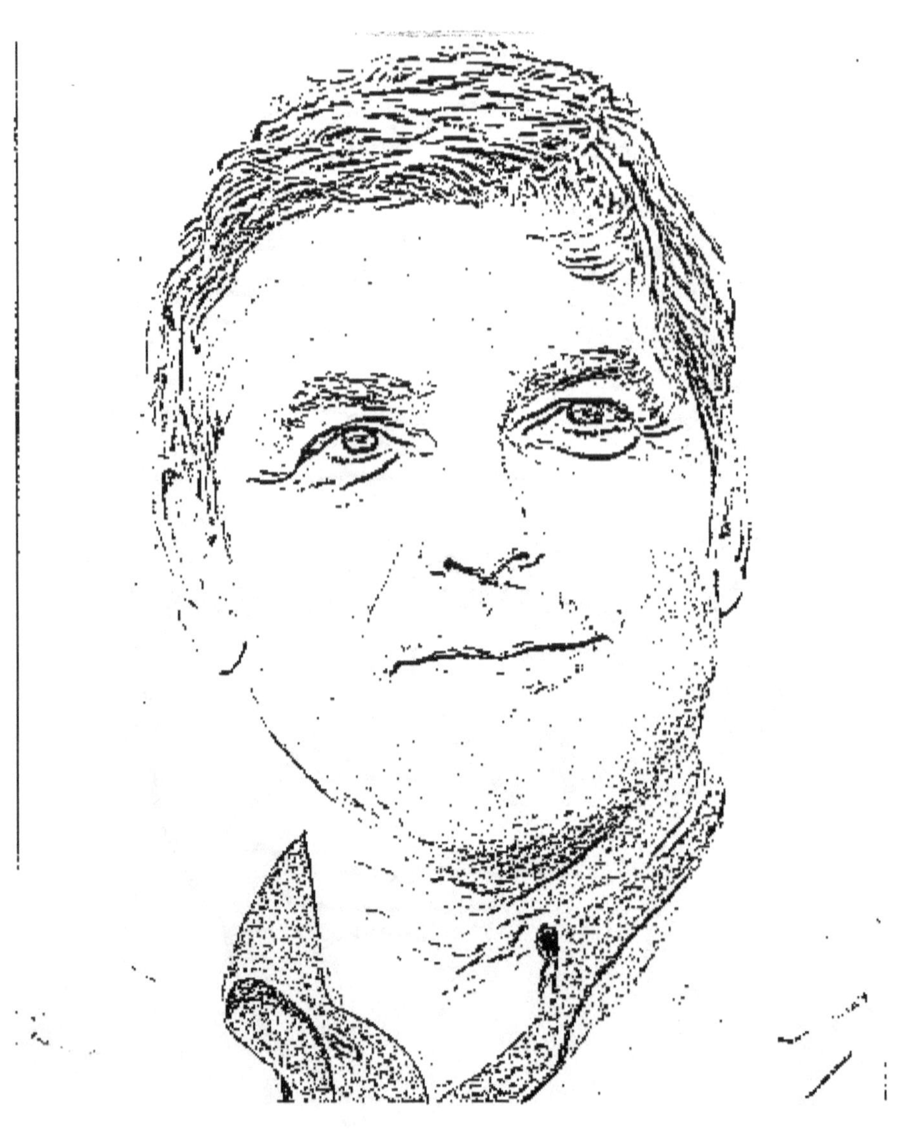

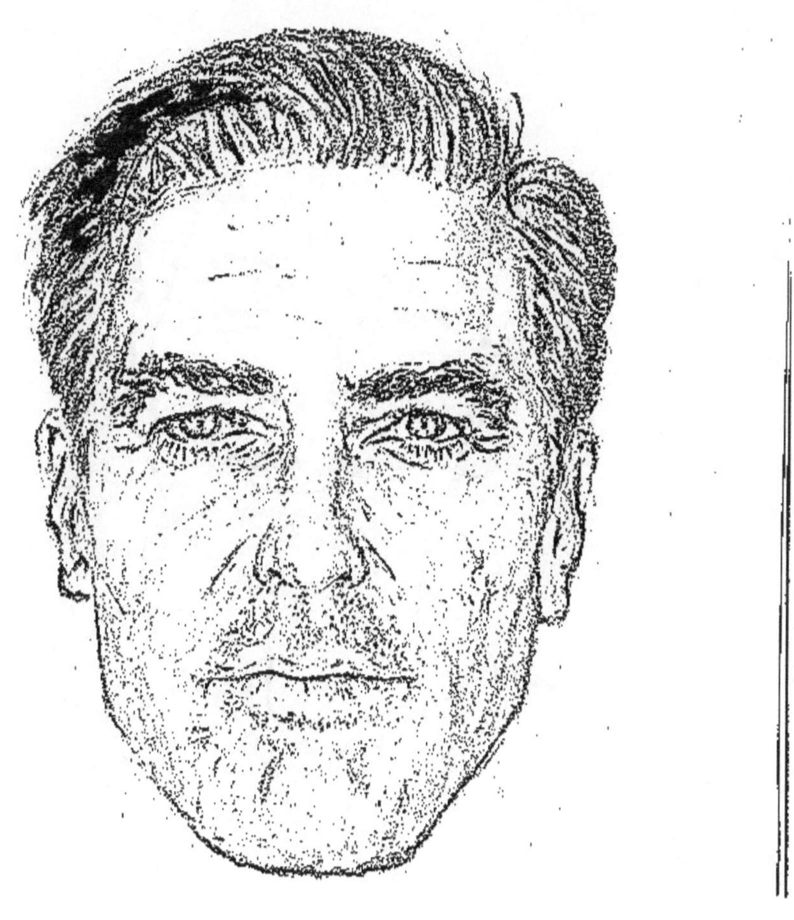

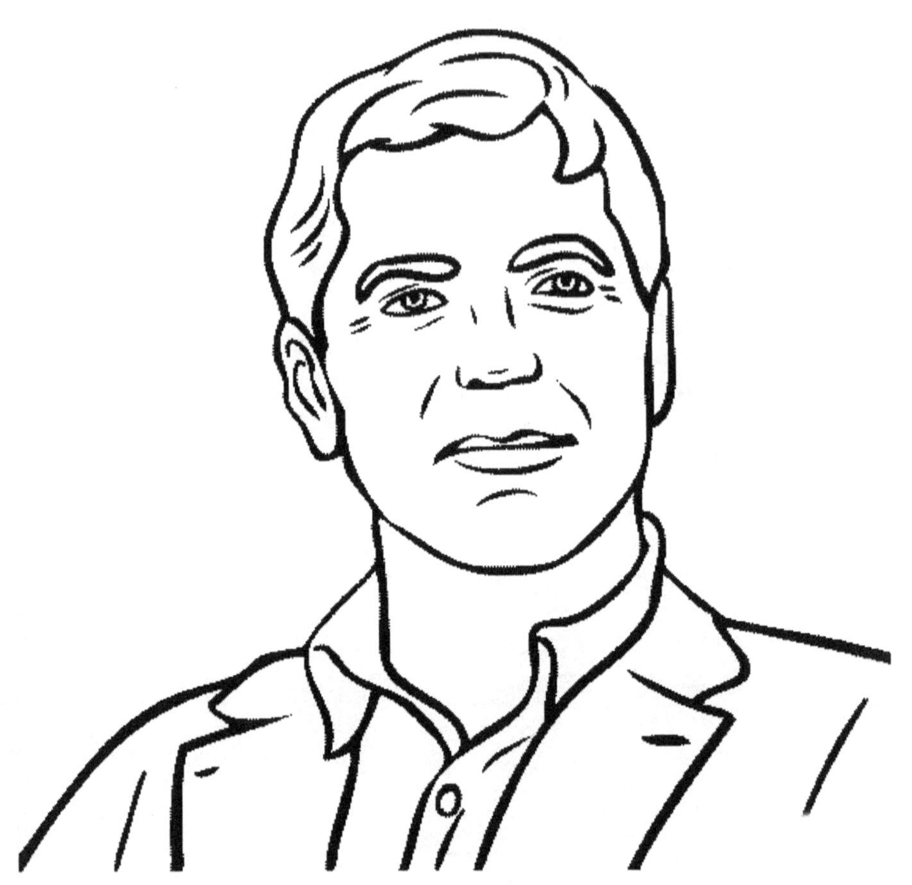

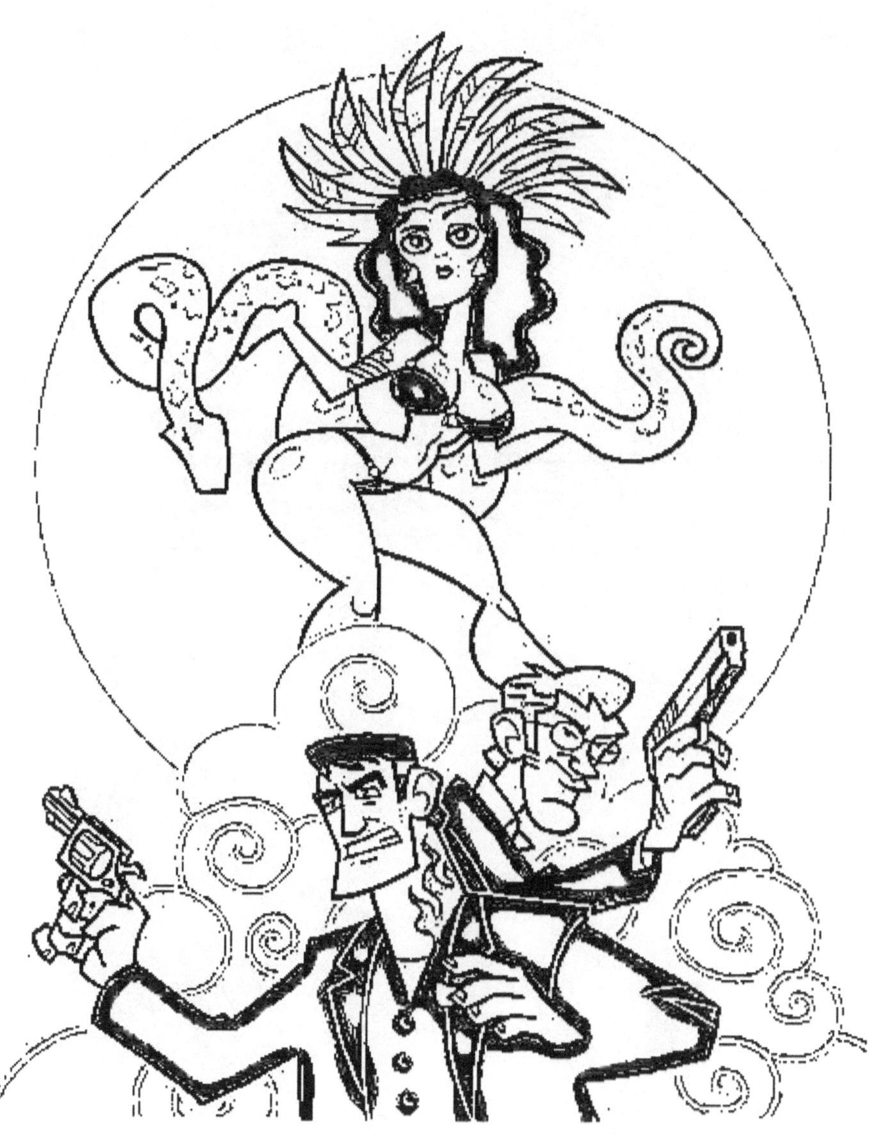

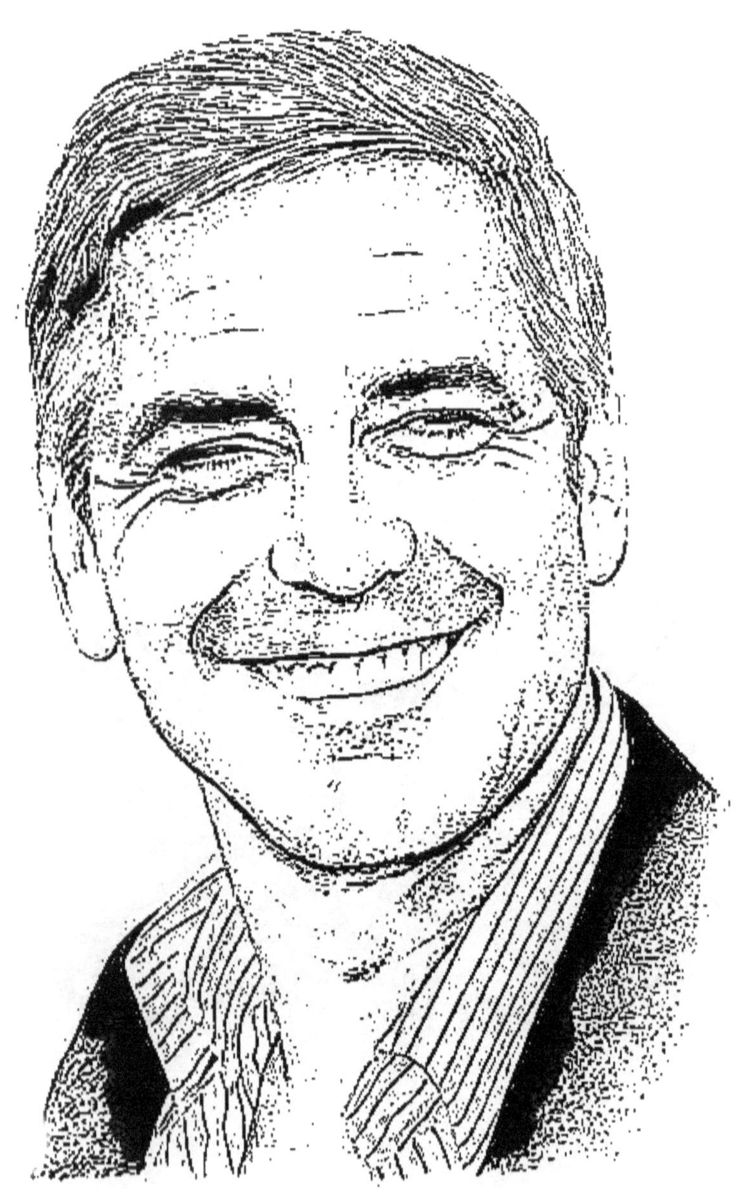

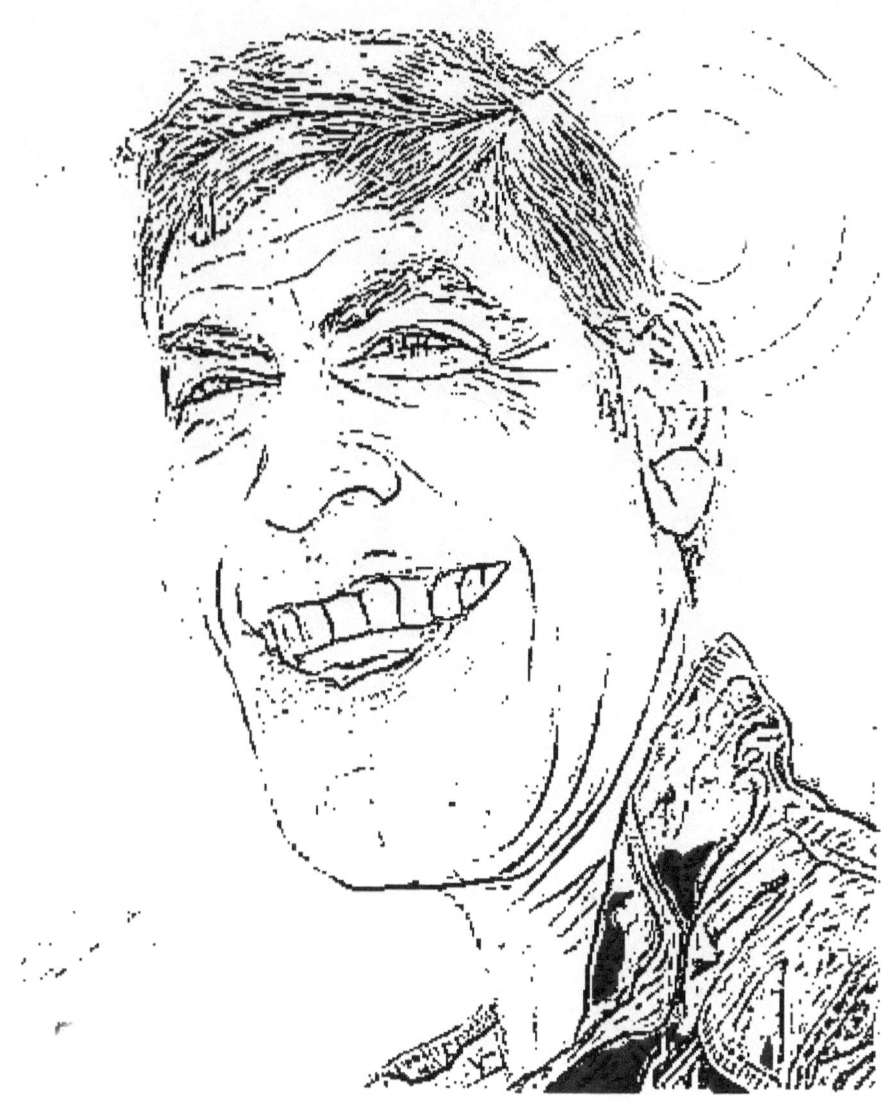

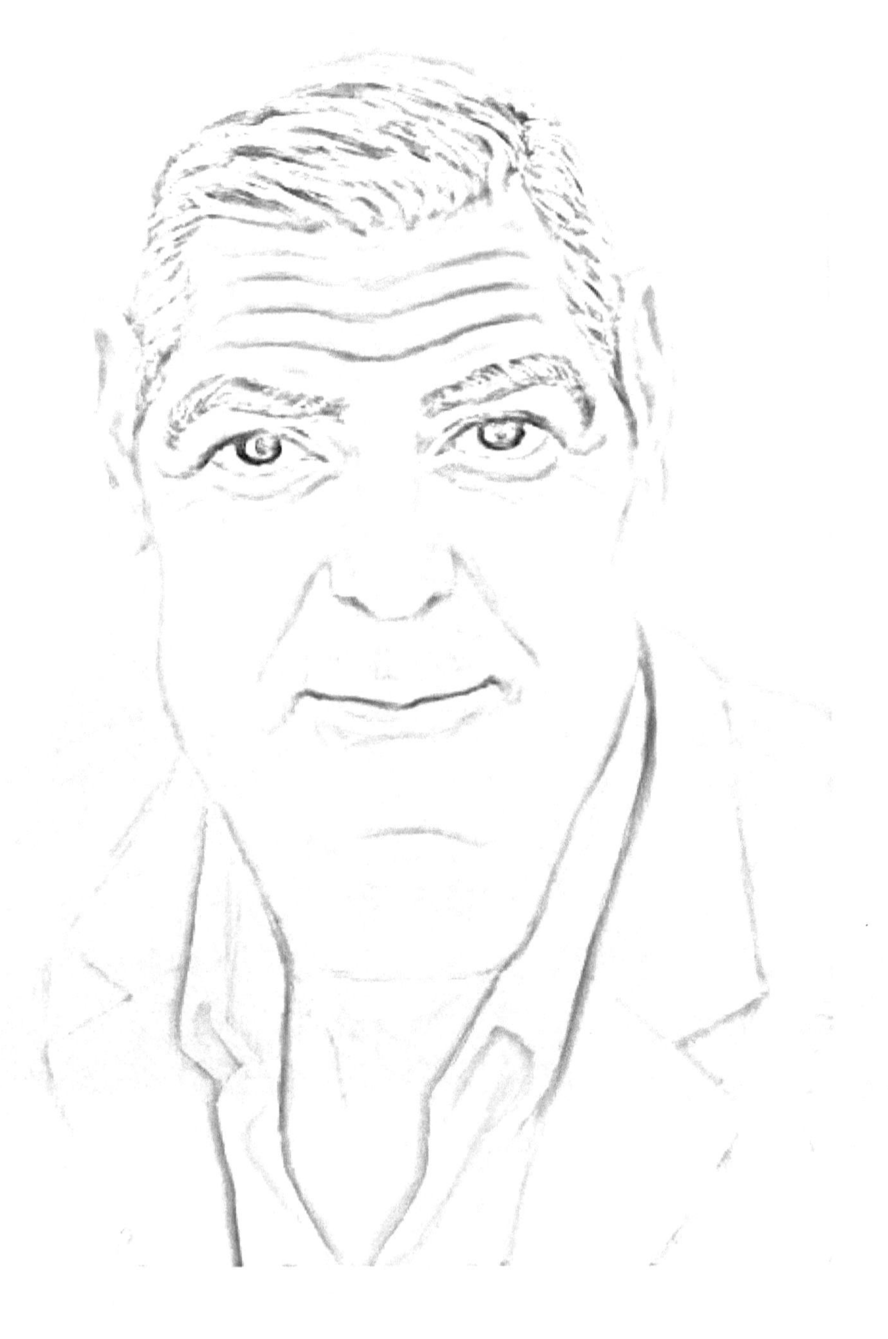

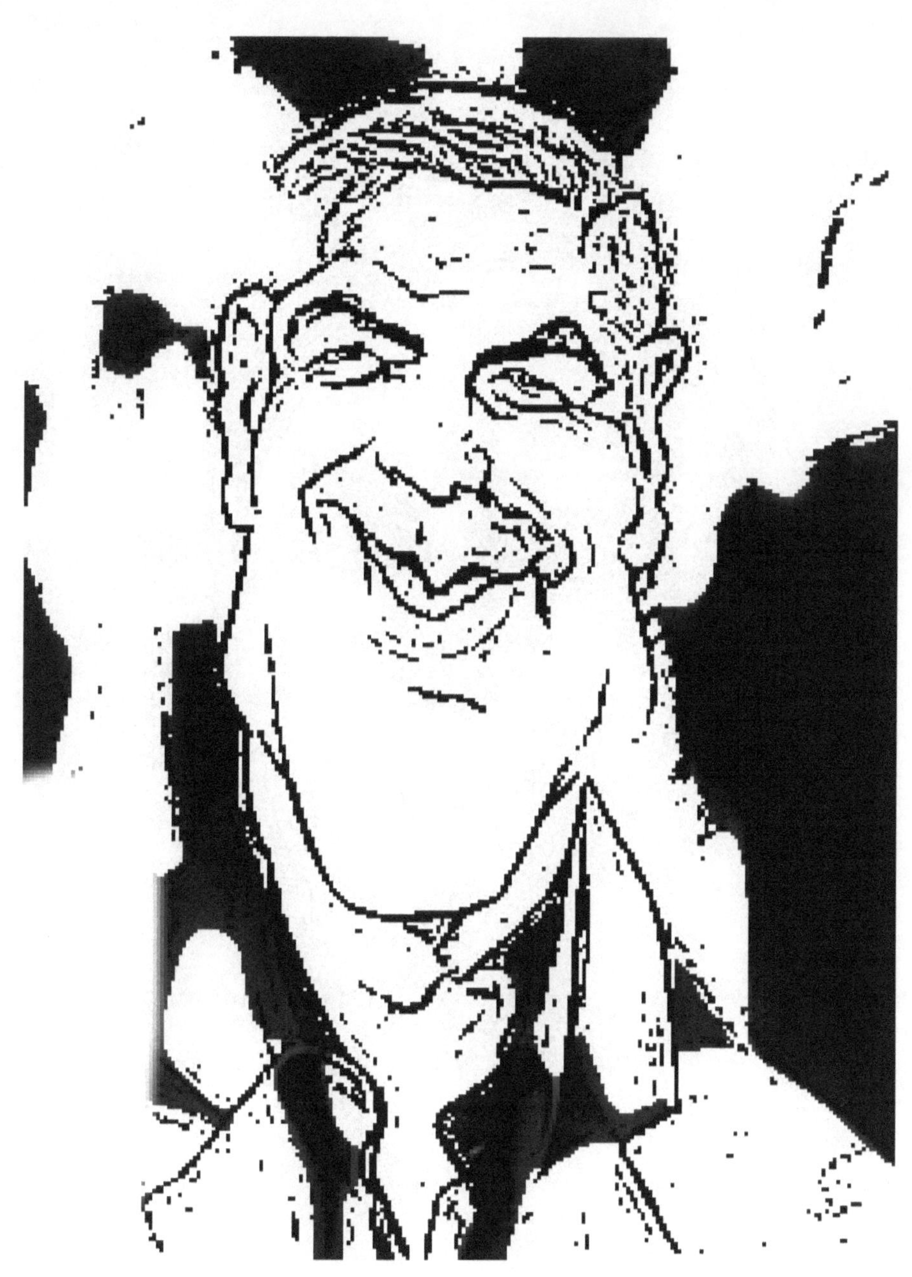

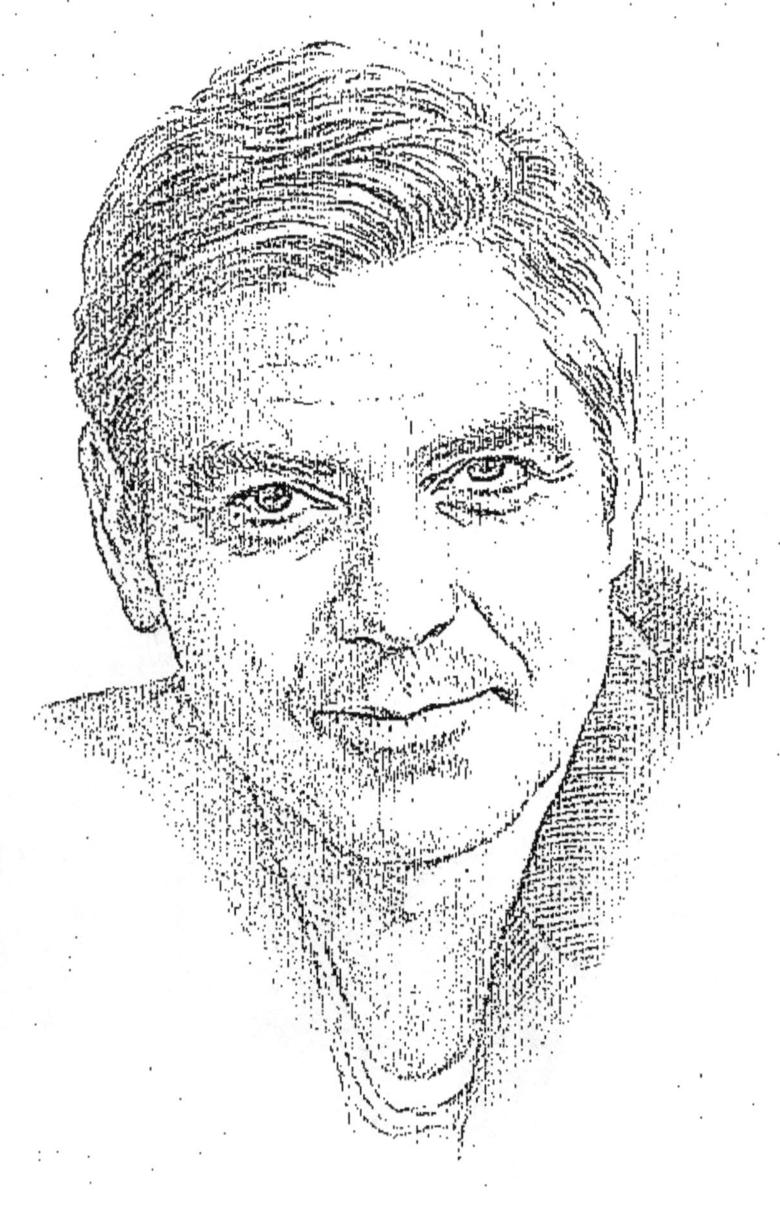

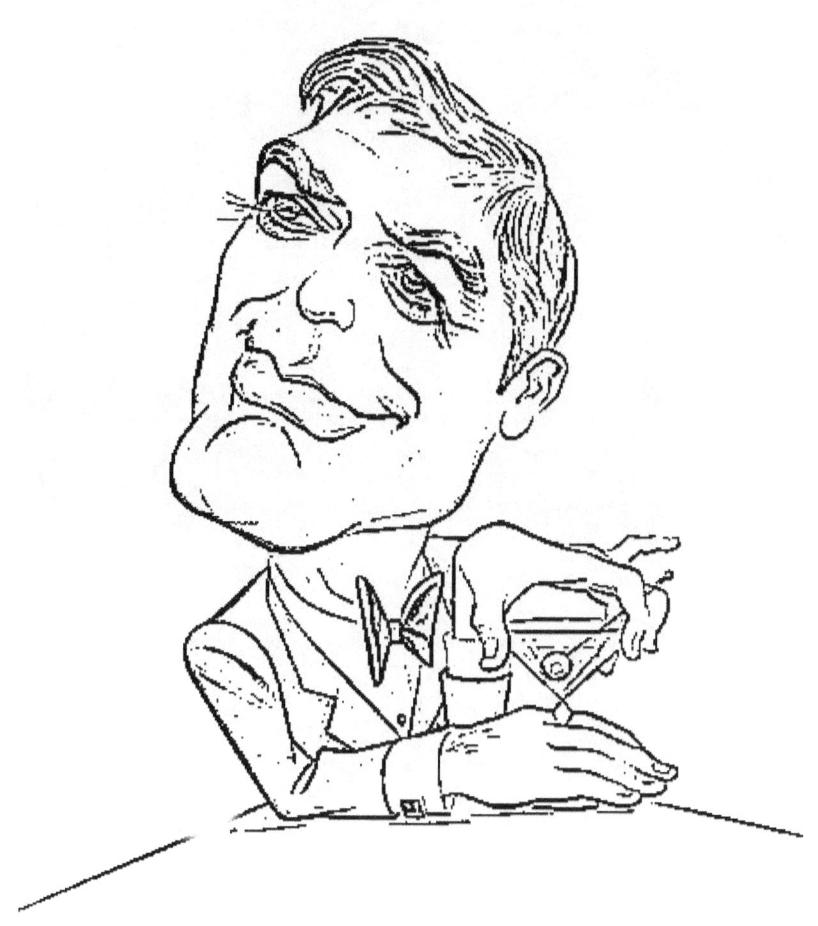

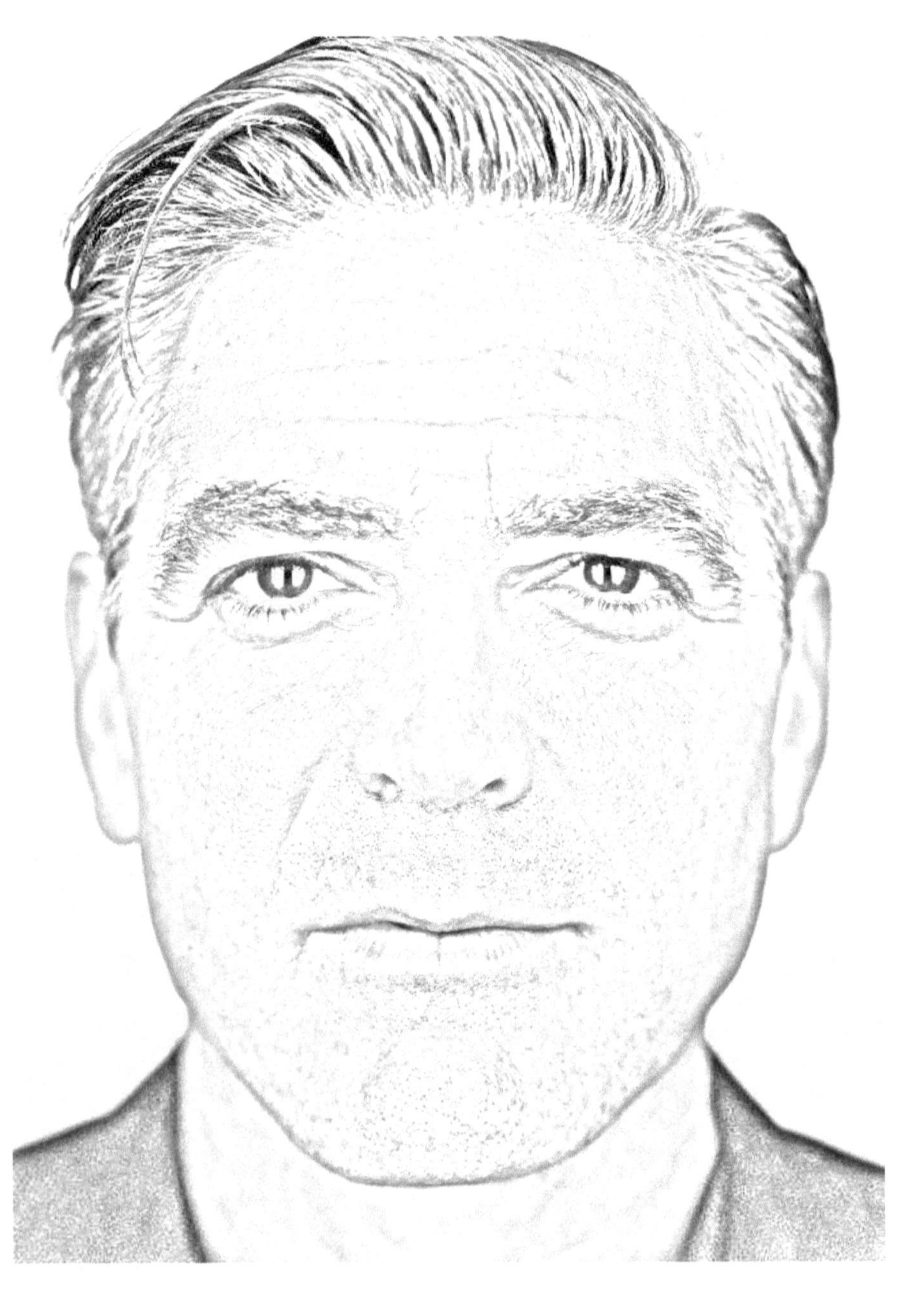

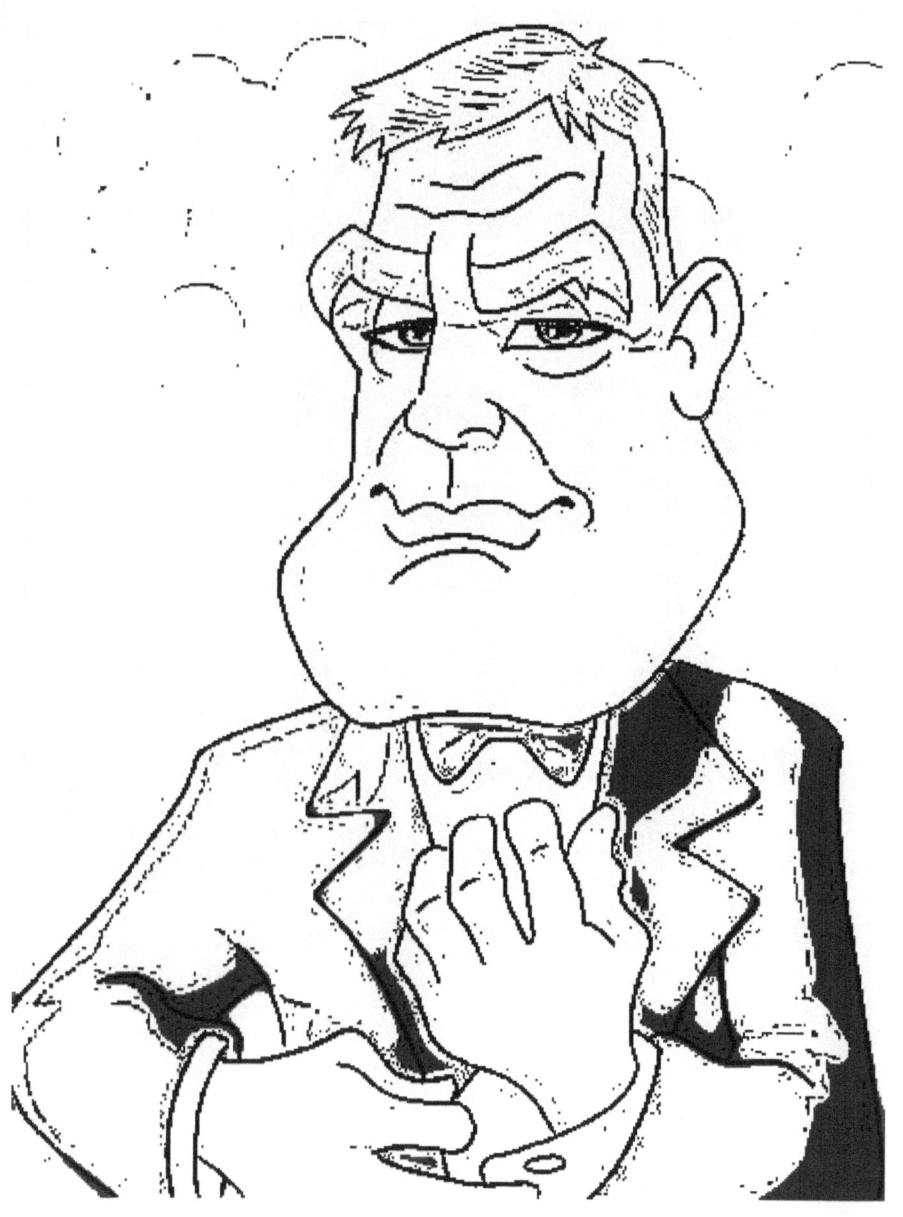

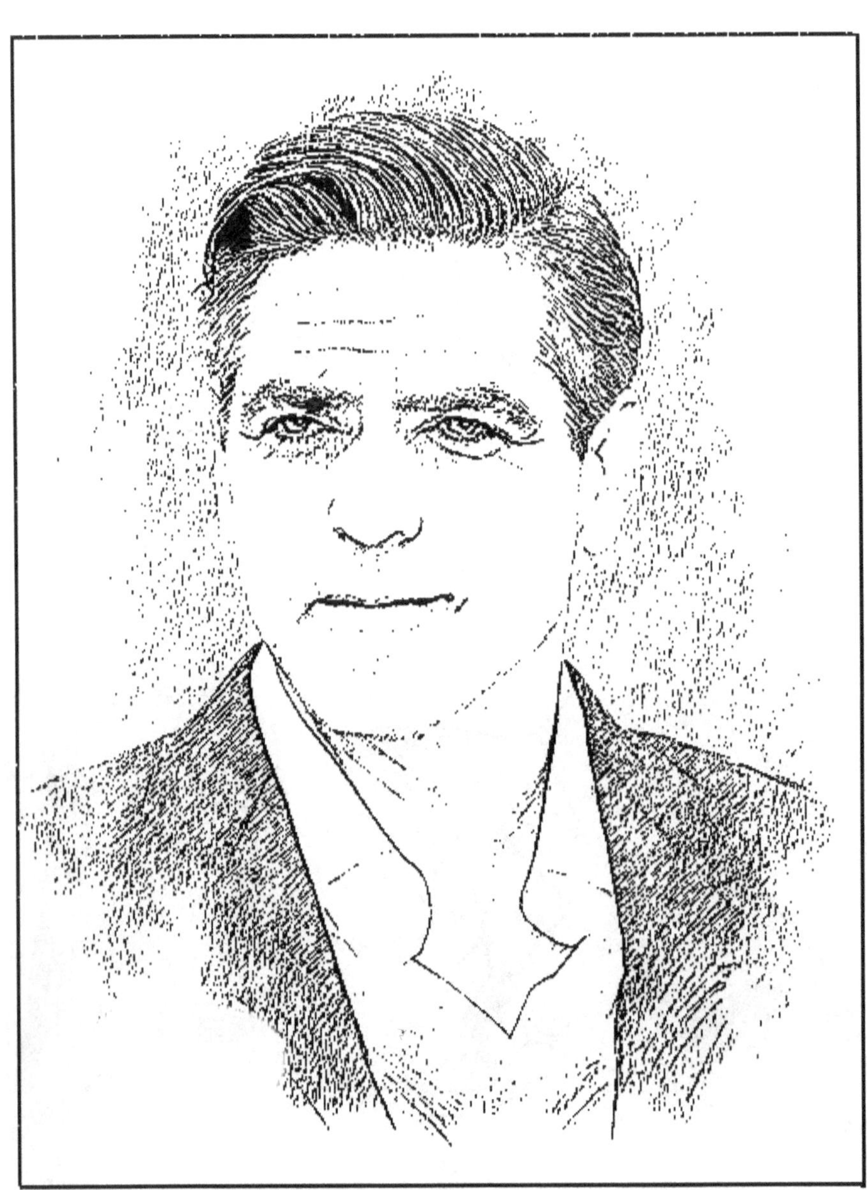

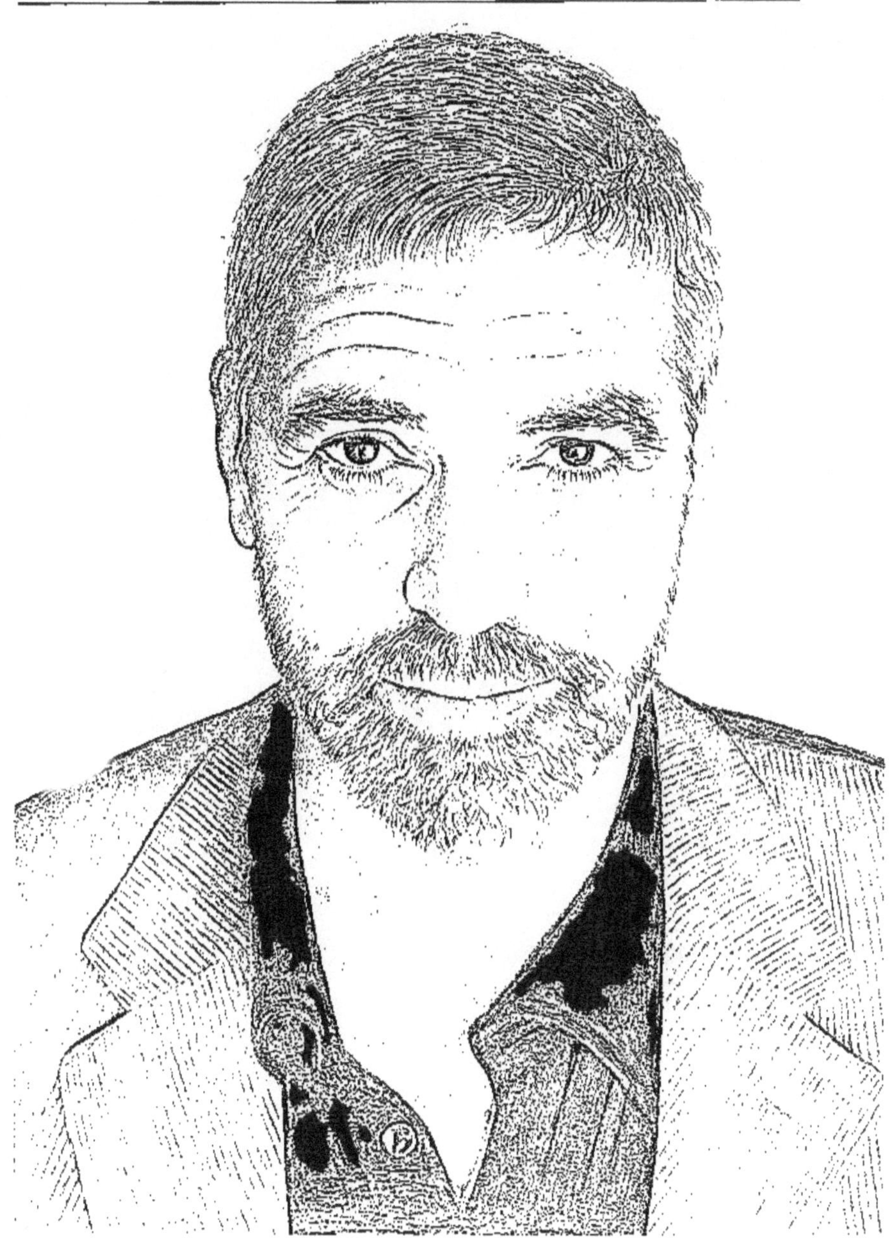